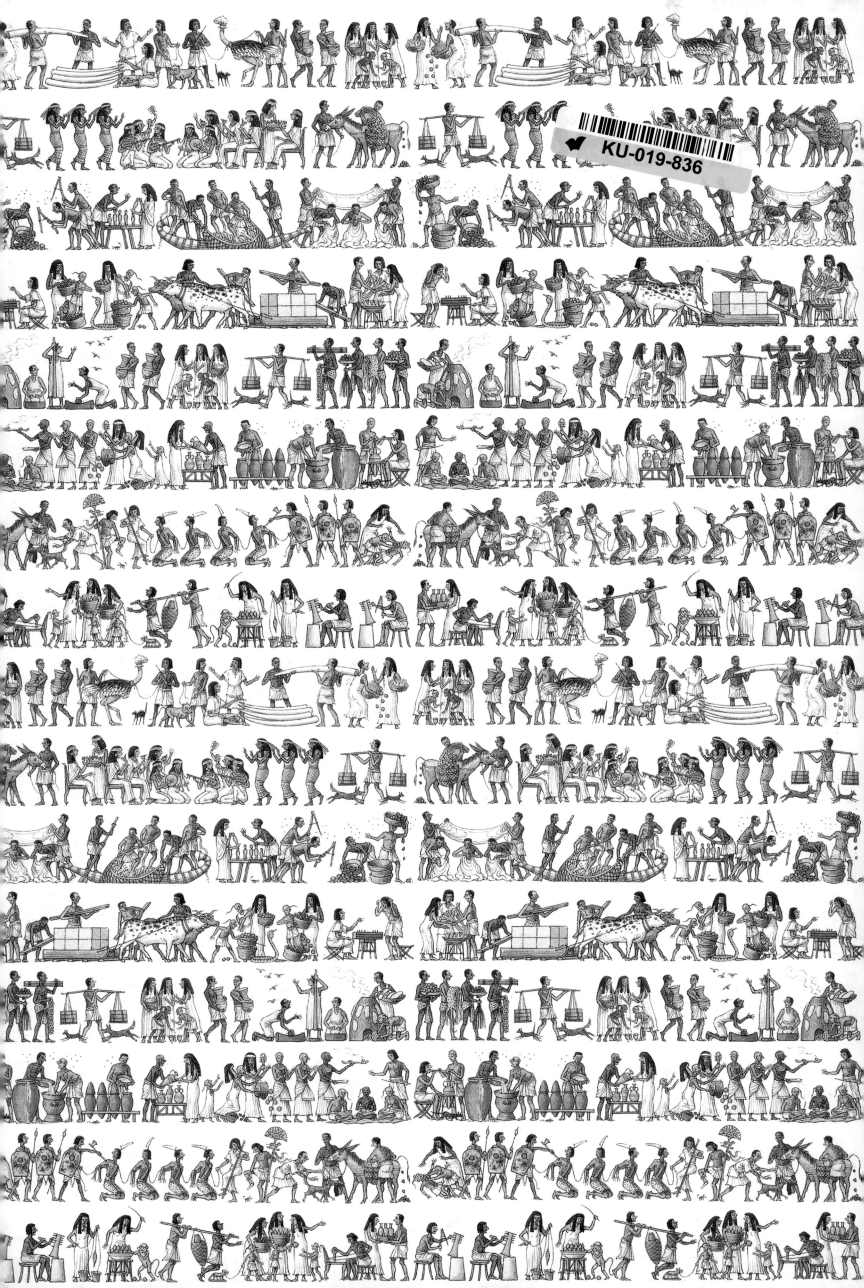

STEPHEN BIESTY

EGYPT

in spectacular cross-section

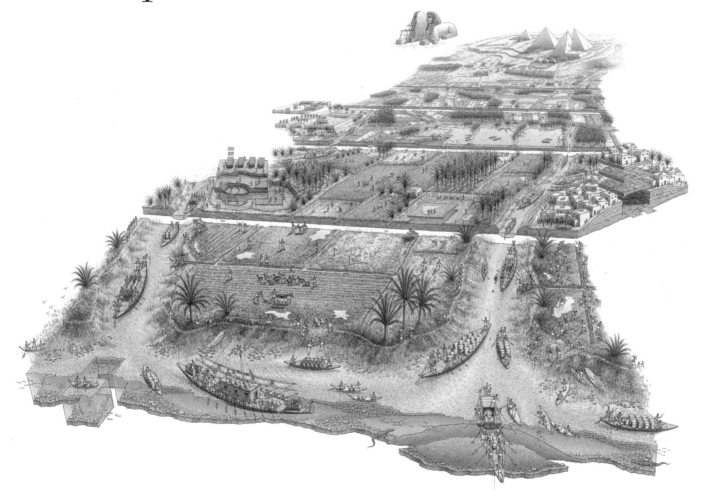

Text by Stewart Ross

Consultants: Delia Pemberton and Joann Fletcher

OXFORD
UNIVERSITY PRESS

'My Land' by Dedia, son of Wennufer

Dedia's family house

Wennufer

Mutnofret,
Dedia's mother

Dedia

Ipuia

Aunt Meritat

In the beginning Atum the Sun god created himself. Later came Nut and Geb, the Heaven and the Earth. And at the centre of the Earth appeared Egypt, the Kingdom of the Two Crowns. It has existed longer than anyone can remember.

This is my land. Watched over by the many gods and goddesses, it is the finest place in all the world. I am very proud of it and cannot imagine what it would be like to be an outsider living elsewhere.

My land is mostly a dry and dusty place. But through the middle runs the Great River, the most important river on Earth. During the winter and spring the River runs lower and lower. But in the summer the God of the Flood causes it to be reborn. It swells, bursting its banks to spread life-giving water over the fields on either side. From these fields come our wealth and our food.

The mighty Rameses, the greatest god-king of all, rules our land. Horus the Falcon God guides him and guards him, and beside him I am nothing but a speck of sand. Just like the River every year and the Sun every morning, after death His Majesty will be reborn. He will then be a god who lives for ever.

We also can be reborn into the Afterlife, the Field of Reeds. To do so we must worship the gods and keep our hearts pure. It's not easy, but I will try. Promise.

Contents

Egypt

the great
River Nile

Our journey

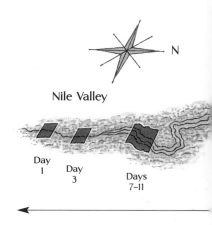

Hello. I'm Dedia, and this is a map of the brilliant adventure I had last year. As I had just turned 11, my dad, Captain Wennufer, said I should learn to help him at work. Delivering cargo as we went, we sailed down the Great River to the wedding of Uncle Nebre in Piramesse. Uncle is a scribe, very rich and important. Mum stayed behind to manage the household. One problem, though: Dad agreed to take my fierce Aunt Meritat and her know-all daughter Ipuia – not my favourite relations.

Nile Valley
Egyptian civilization flourished within the valley cut by the mighty River Nile as it snaked through the arid desert. In September, as the river's annual flood is subsiding, the river is still several metres deep and flowing as fast as a boy can run.

DAY 11

cemetery
The last rites are being performed for the village's respected head man.

DAY 10

Deir el-Medina
The crowded village has been built to house workers from the Valley of the Kings.

friend's house

DAY 1

Elephantine
The journey starts here – the furthest south boats can sail without meeting rapids.

Valley of the Queens

Wennufer's ship

Dedia's house

First cataract

desert

Thebes

edge of desert

DAY 18

farmland
Rich farmland is visible o both banks of the river.

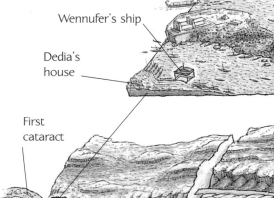

quarry

tomb of Rameses II

DAY 3

Gebel el-Silsila
The stone from this quarry provides building material for use all over Egypt.

DAY 7

Karnak
Beside the broad waters of the Nile lies the most glorious temple in all Egypt.

Temple of Amun

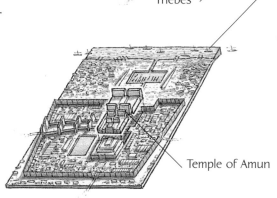

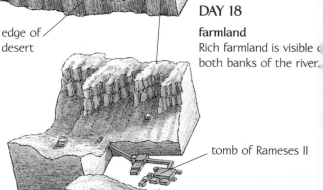

DAY 10

Valley of the Kings
In this secret site of royal burials craftsmen are preparing a tomb for our king, His Majesty Rameses II.

Nile Delta

Day 18
Day 22
Day 24
Day 30

800 km
500 miles

The Egyptian calendar

The 360 normal days of the Egyptian year were divided into 12 equal months:

year   month   day

and into three seasons:

Inundation   winter   summer

Numbers were built up using symbols, an upside-down horseshoe representing 10. The calendar started afresh with each new reign. So 1278 BCE, the second year of the reign of Rameses II, was written like this:

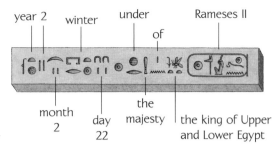

year 2   winter   under   of   Rameses II

month 2   day 22   the majesty   the king of Upper and Lower Egypt

Our story is set in the 48th year of the reign of Rameses II (1230 BCE).

DAY 24

Giza
The famous monuments of Giza are visible beyond the rich farmland of the riverbank.

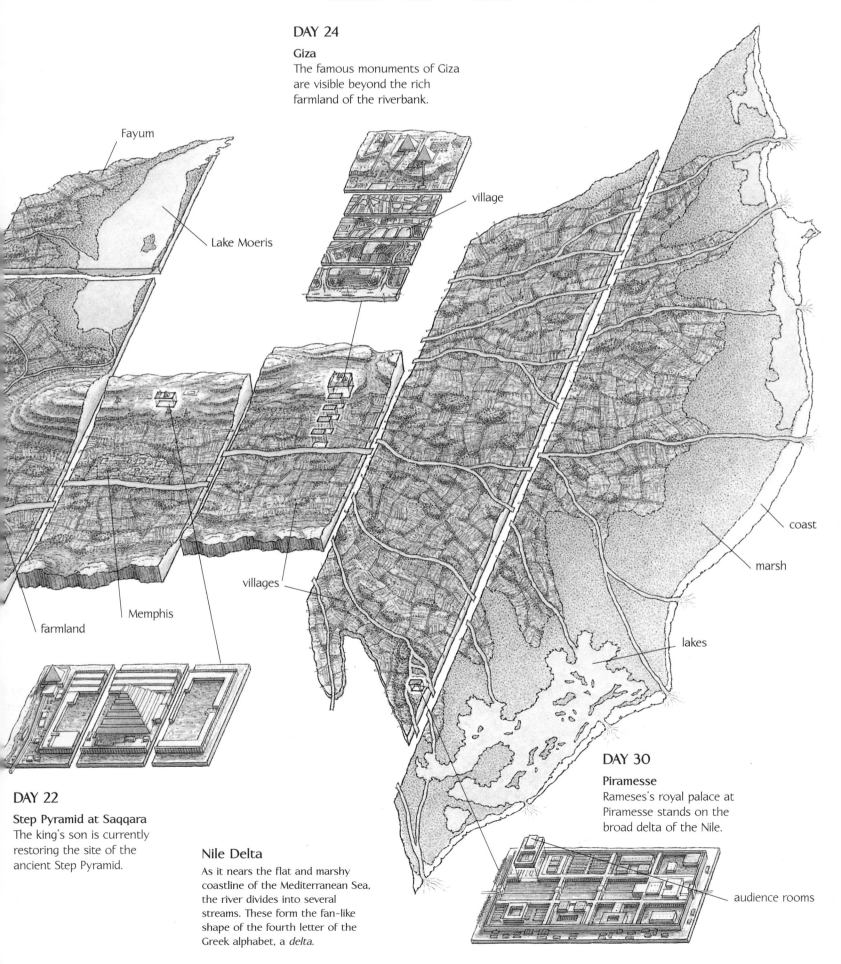

Fayum

Lake Moeris

village

villages

farmland

Memphis

coast

marsh

lakes

DAY 22

Step Pyramid at Saqqara
The king's son is currently restoring the site of the ancient Step Pyramid.

Nile Delta
As it nears the flat and marshy coastline of the Mediterranean Sea, the river divides into several streams. These form the fan-like shape of the fourth letter of the Greek alphabet, a *delta*.

DAY 30

Piramesse
Rameses's royal palace at Piramesse stands on the broad delta of the Nile.

audience rooms

The harbour at Elephantine

I'd often visited the docks at Elephantine, but only to watch. This time it was for real – I was actually setting off for Lower Egypt, the kingdom of the Red Crown. Feeling anxious, I clutched the amulet Mum had given me. I needed the gods' protection. One wish came true straightaway. Aunt Meritat and Cousin Ipuia were late. To keep to his tight schedule, Dad left without them. Hooray!

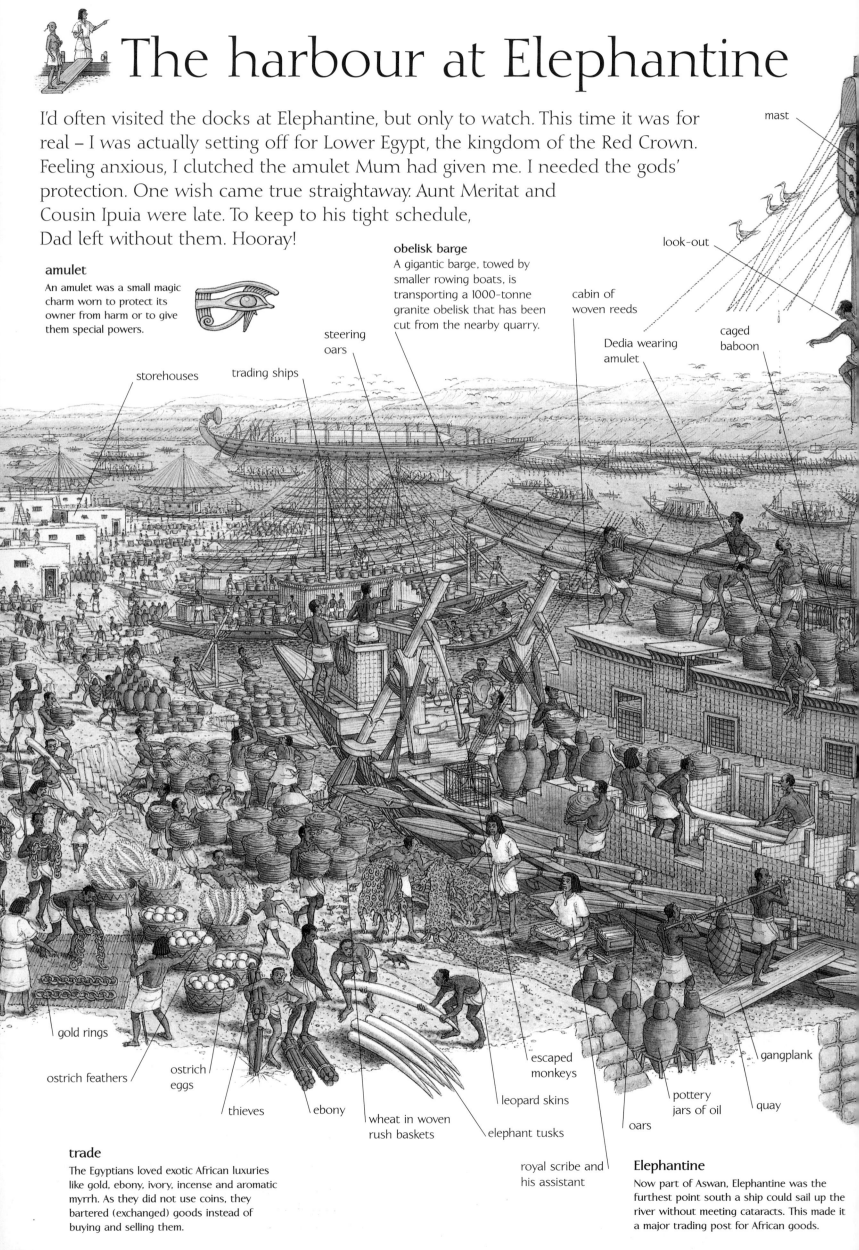

amulet
An amulet was a small magic charm worn to protect its owner from harm or to give them special powers.

obelisk barge
A gigantic barge, towed by smaller rowing boats, is transporting a 1000-tonne granite obelisk that has been cut from the nearby quarry.

mast

look-out

steering oars

cabin of woven reeds

caged baboon

Dedia wearing amulet

storehouses

trading ships

gold rings

ostrich feathers

ostrich eggs

thieves

ebony

wheat in woven rush baskets

escaped monkeys

leopard skins

elephant tusks

gangplank

pottery jars of oil

oars

quay

royal scribe and his assistant

trade
The Egyptians loved exotic African luxuries like gold, ebony, ivory, incense and aromatic myrrh. As they did not use coins, they bartered (exchanged) goods instead of buying and selling them.

Elephantine
Now part of Aswan, Elephantine was the furthest point south a ship could sail up the river without meeting cataracts. This made it a major trading post for African goods.

10

cataracts
The first of the Nile's six cataracts – rocky rapids impassable to ships – was just south of Elephantine. At a cataract a ship was hauled from the river and dragged to the next stretch of smooth water.

rope made from plant fibres

Nilometer
Nilometers accurately measure the height of the river. This one consists of steps which the water covers or reveals as it rises and falls. Nilometers may have been used to estimate taxes – a high flood might mean more arable land the next harvest, so increased taxes!

wealthy lady in her private barge

temple of Khnum
The ram-headed potter god Khnum is Elephantine's main deity. Because rams are associated with fertility and potters with making things, Khnum is also seen as a creator god.

Khnum

Day 1

rowers

palm trees

prisoners of war

ship's toilet

mud-sealed jars of incense

Wennufer

dom nuts

stone ballast to keep the ship upright

ship construction
Ships were made of long planks tied together over a skeleton of beams. Rectangular linen sails, mainly used for upstream travel, were hung between two wooden spars. Oars made the boat faster and helped with steering.

Quarrying at Gebel el-Silsila

Our first stop was the Gebel el-Silsila stone quarries. While the stores were being unloaded, I wandered up to the quarry face. The skill of the workmen – many only slaves – was amazing. Imagine hacking out a block of stone exactly square – incredible! On my return, bad news: Aunt Meritat had taken another boat and caught us up. Worse still, Ipuia had brought along the most inconvenient wedding present. A live lion cub.

sailing upstream

baskets of grain – the workers' wages

Wennufer organizing the unloading of cargo

quay

singing
The oarsmen sing to help keep the rhythm of their rowing.

stone blocks being taken downstream

slavery
Slaves were normally prisoners of war. They were not necessarily badly treated. Many worked as household servants, and fortunate ones even owned their own land.

ferry

papyrus skiff

fishing
Fishing is an uncertain business. Some fish may not be caught because they are sacred – and the situation varies from region to region.

hippo

hippo hunt
Hippo hunting is a popular activity, although only males are supposed to be killed. The female hippo is associated with the household goddess Taweret, known as 'the great female'.

crocodile attack
Attack by Nile crocodiles is a real danger. Nevertheless, killing a crocodile is not approved of in areas that worship the crocodile god Sobek.

maid with ostrich-feather fan

lion cub

Aunt Meritat

Ipuia

Dedia

roast gazelle

linen awning

ramp

tools
In Dedia's time tools were made of stone, wood or bronze, a mixture of copper (about 90–95%) and tin (about 5–10%). A bronze chisel soon went blunt when it was hammered into stone.

sledge and levers

mason's mallet

wooden wedge

stone pounder

bronze or copper chisels

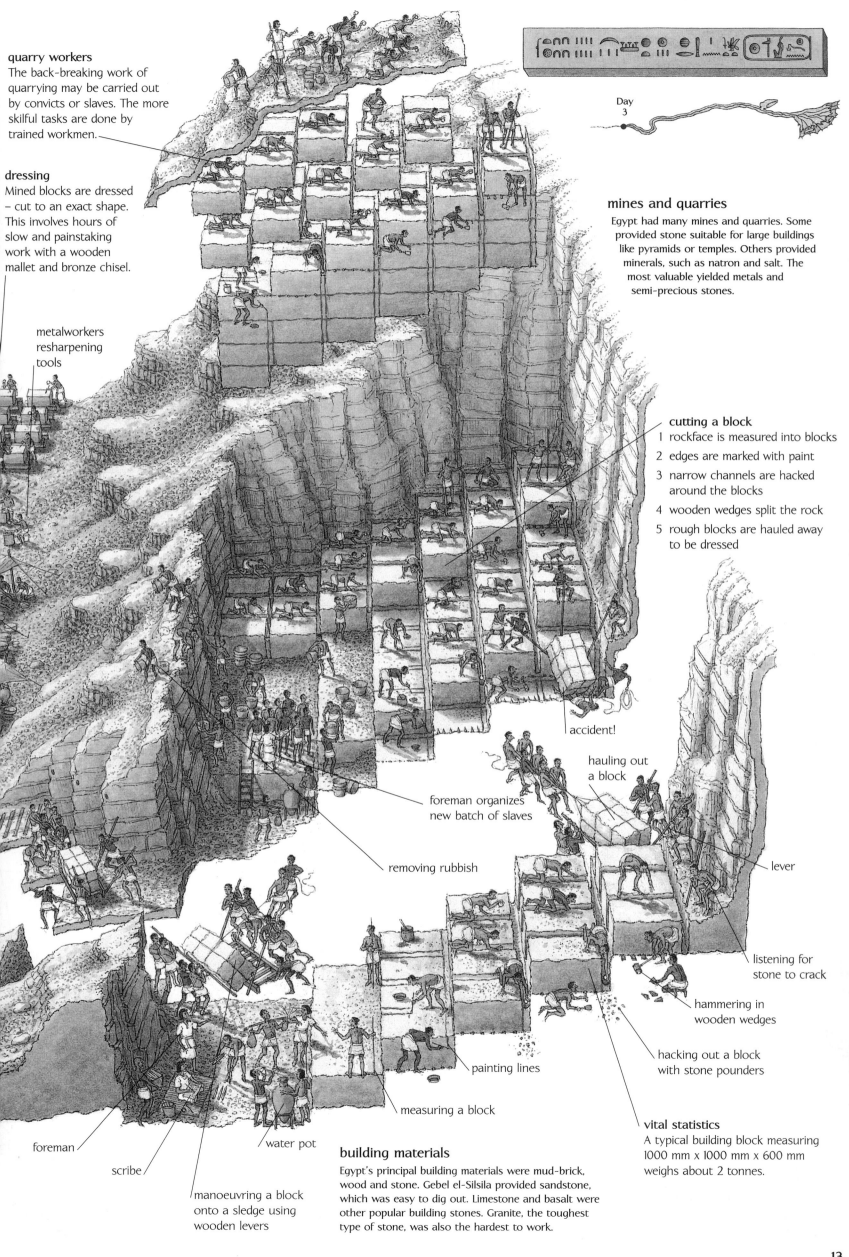

quarry workers
The back-breaking work of quarrying may be carried out by convicts or slaves. The more skilful tasks are done by trained workmen.

dressing
Mined blocks are dressed – cut to an exact shape. This involves hours of slow and painstaking work with a wooden mallet and bronze chisel.

metalworkers resharpening tools

mines and quarries
Egypt had many mines and quarries. Some provided stone suitable for large buildings like pyramids or temples. Others provided minerals, such as natron and salt. The most valuable yielded metals and semi-precious stones.

cutting a block
1 rockface is measured into blocks
2 edges are marked with paint
3 narrow channels are hacked around the blocks
4 wooden wedges split the rock
5 rough blocks are hauled away to be dressed

accident!

hauling out a block

foreman organizes new batch of slaves

removing rubbish

lever

listening for stone to crack

hammering in wooden wedges

painting lines

hacking out a block with stone pounders

measuring a block

water pot

foreman

scribe

manoeuvring a block onto a sledge using wooden levers

building materials
Egypt's principal building materials were mud-brick, wood and stone. Gebel el-Silsila provided sandstone, which was easy to dig out. Limestone and basalt were other popular building stones. Granite, the toughest type of stone, was also the hardest to work.

vital statistics
A typical building block measuring 1000 mm x 1000 mm x 600 mm weighs about 2 tonnes.

13

Amun-Ra's temple at Karnak

The temple at Karnak, our next stop, was awe-inspiring. It made me feel so small. We sensed the mighty Amun-Ra everywhere, as if he were watching us. Ipuia and I went with Dad to deliver the gold, ivory and leopard skins to the temple storeman. To lighten the atmosphere a bit, I asked the storeman if he'd like the skin of a lion cub, too. Sadly, he said no. Ipuia was livid!

obelisk of Thutmose III
Kings like Thutmose III erected obelisks to emphasize their link to the Sun god. The obelisk, with its gilded tip, points to the Sun. The base is carved with baboons, creatures famous for getting very excited at sunrise.

shrine
A temple is a god or goddess's house, so Amun-Ra lives in the temple at Karnak. He actually resides in the shrine (or sanctuary), at the very heart of the temple, where his statue is kept.

priests
Priests, who are not necessarily learned or holy, are servants at the house of Amun-Ra. Their job may be inherited. They live by strict rules, but most work in the temple only one month in every four.

obelisk of Thutmose I

pylon of Thutmose I and III

pylon of Thutmose I

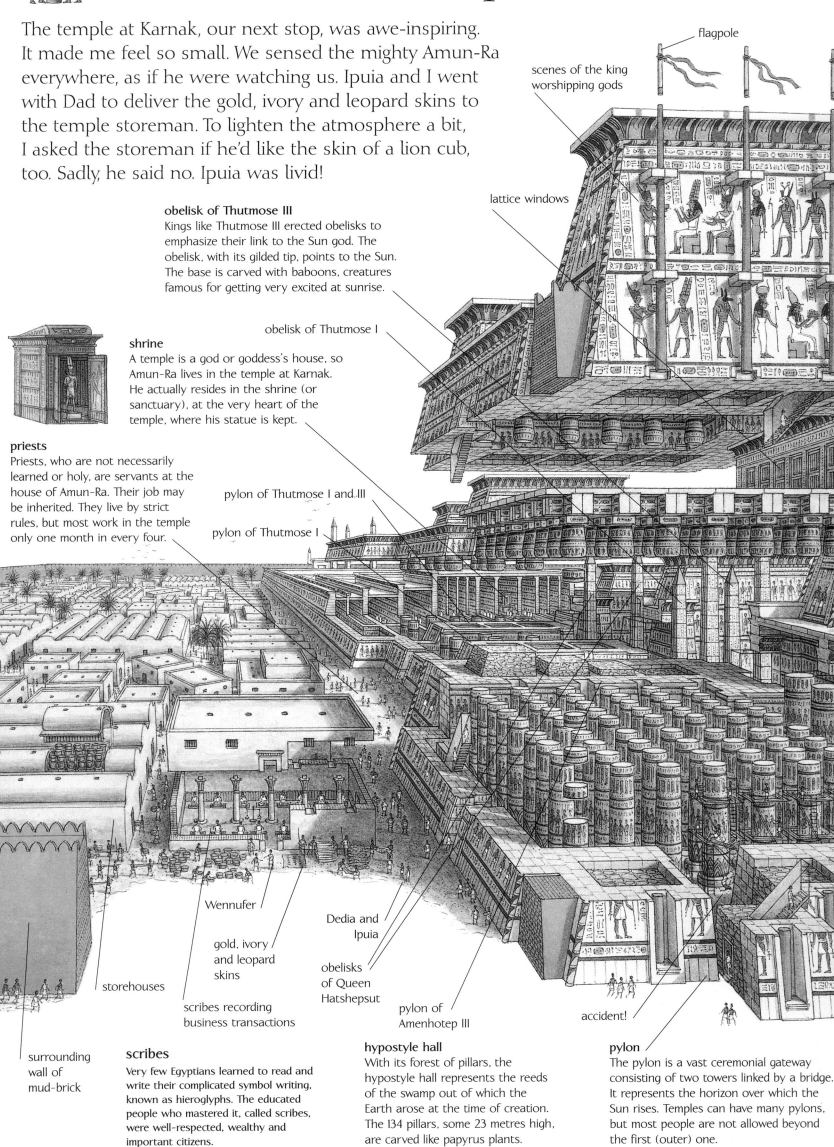

flagpole

scenes of the king worshipping gods

lattice windows

surrounding wall of mud-brick

storehouses

Wennufer

gold, ivory and leopard skins

scribes recording business transactions

Dedia and Ipuia

obelisks of Queen Hatshepsut

pylon of Amenhotep III

accident!

pylon

scribes
Very few Egyptians learned to read and write their complicated symbol writing, known as hieroglyphs. The educated people who mastered it, called scribes, were well-respected, wealthy and important citizens.

hypostyle hall
With its forest of pillars, the hypostyle hall represents the reeds of the swamp out of which the Earth arose at the time of creation. The 134 pillars, some 23 metres high, are carved like papyrus plants.

pylon
The pylon is a vast ceremonial gateway consisting of two towers linked by a bridge. It represents the horizon over which the Sun rises. Temples can have many pylons, but most people are not allowed beyond the first (outer) one.

14

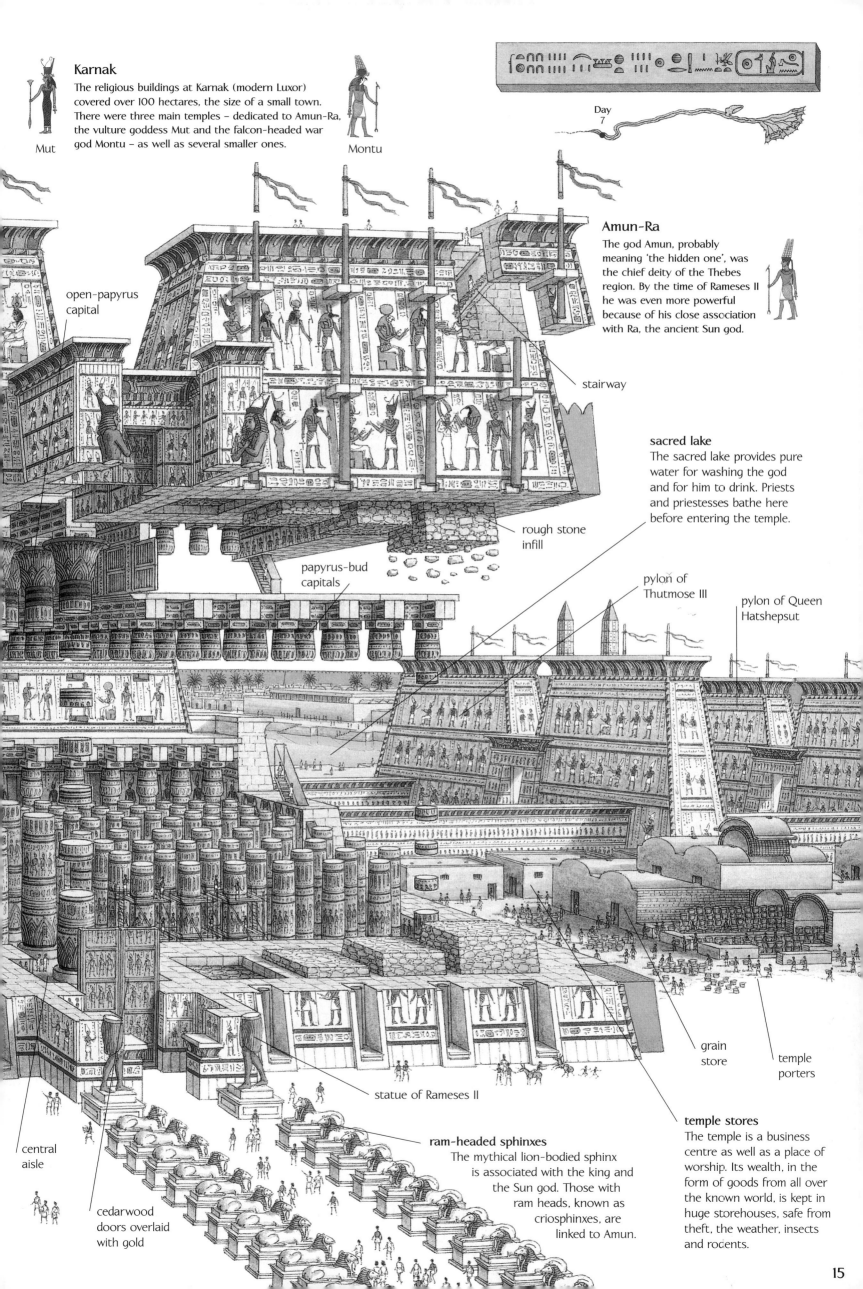

Karnak

The religious buildings at Karnak (modern Luxor) covered over 100 hectares, the size of a small town. There were three main temples – dedicated to Amun-Ra, the vulture goddess Mut and the falcon-headed war god Montu – as well as several smaller ones.

Mut

Montu

Day 7

Amun-Ra

The god Amun, probably meaning 'the hidden one', was the chief deity of the Thebes region. By the time of Rameses II he was even more powerful because of his close association with Ra, the ancient Sun god.

open-papyrus capital

stairway

sacred lake
The sacred lake provides pure water for washing the god and for him to drink. Priests and priestesses bathe here before entering the temple.

rough stone infill

papyrus-bud capitals

pylon of Thutmose III

pylon of Queen Hatshepsut

statue of Rameses II

grain store

temple porters

central aisle

cedarwood doors overlaid with gold

ram-headed sphinxes
The mythical lion-bodied sphinx is associated with the king and the Sun god. Those with ram heads, known as criosphinxes, are linked to Amun.

temple stores
The temple is a business centre as well as a place of worship. Its wealth, in the form of goods from all over the known world, is kept in huge storehouses, safe from theft, the weather, insects and rodents.

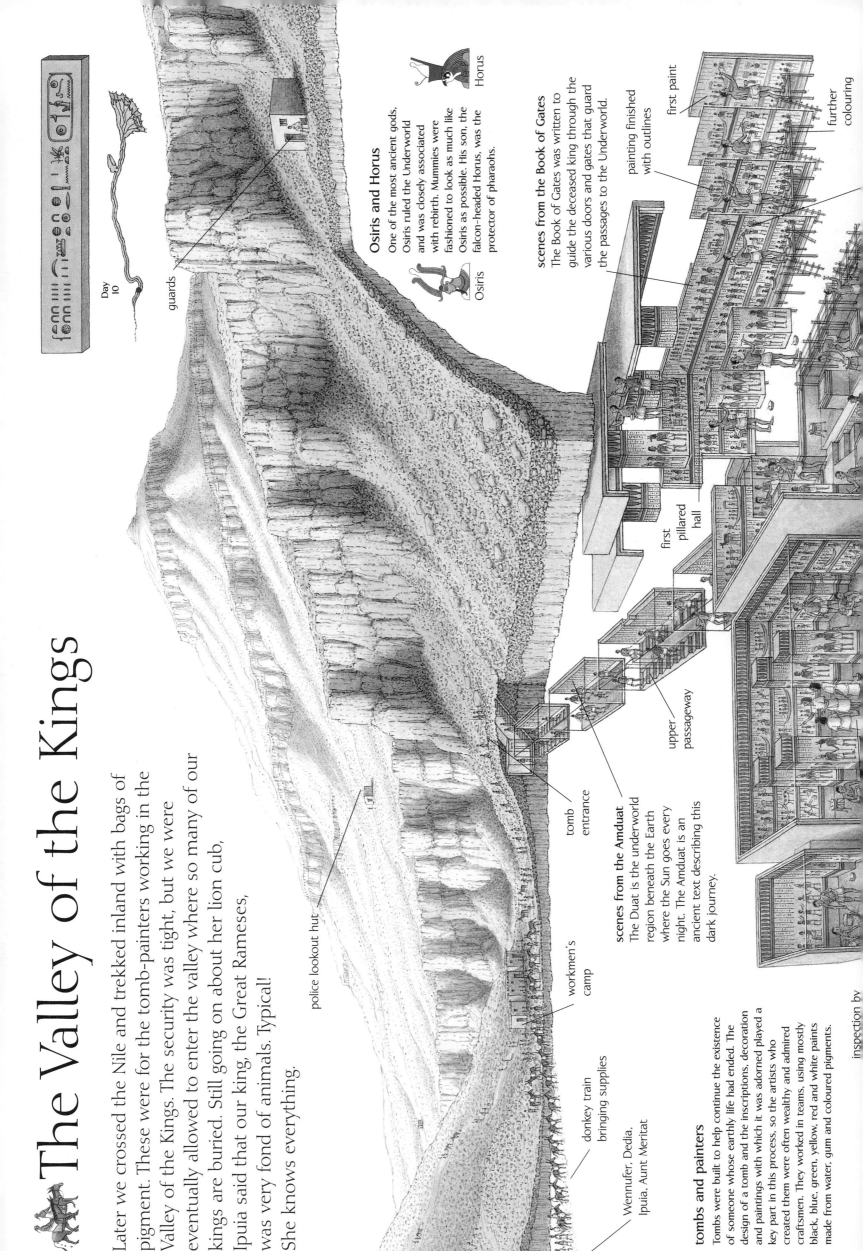

The Valley of the Kings

Later we crossed the Nile and trekked inland with bags of pigment. These were for the tomb-painters working in the Valley of the Kings. The security was tight, but we were eventually allowed to enter the valley where so many of our kings are buried. Still going on about her lion cub, Ipuia said that our king, the Great Rameses, was very fond of animals. Typical! She knows everything.

Day 10

guards

police lookout hut

workmen's camp

donkey train bringing supplies

Wennufer, Dedia, Ipuia, Aunt Meritat

Osiris and Horus

One of the most ancient gods, Osiris ruled the Underworld and was closely associated with rebirth. Mummies were fashioned to look as much like Osiris as possible. His son, the falcon-headed Horus, was the protector of pharaohs.

Horus

Osiris

scenes from the Book of Gates

The Book of Gates was written to guide the deceased king through the various doors and gates that guard the passages to the Underworld.

painting finished with outlines

first paint

further colouring

first pillared hall

upper passageway

tomb entrance

scenes from the Amduat

The Duat is the underworld region beneath the Earth where the Sun goes every night. The Amduat is an ancient text describing this dark journey.

tombs and painters

Tombs were built to help continue the existence of someone whose earthly life had ended. The design of a tomb and the inscriptions, decoration and paintings with which it was adorned played a key part in this process, so the artists who created them were often wealthy and admired craftsmen. They worked in teams, using mostly black, blue, green, yellow, red and white paints made from water, gum and coloured pigments.

inspection by

16

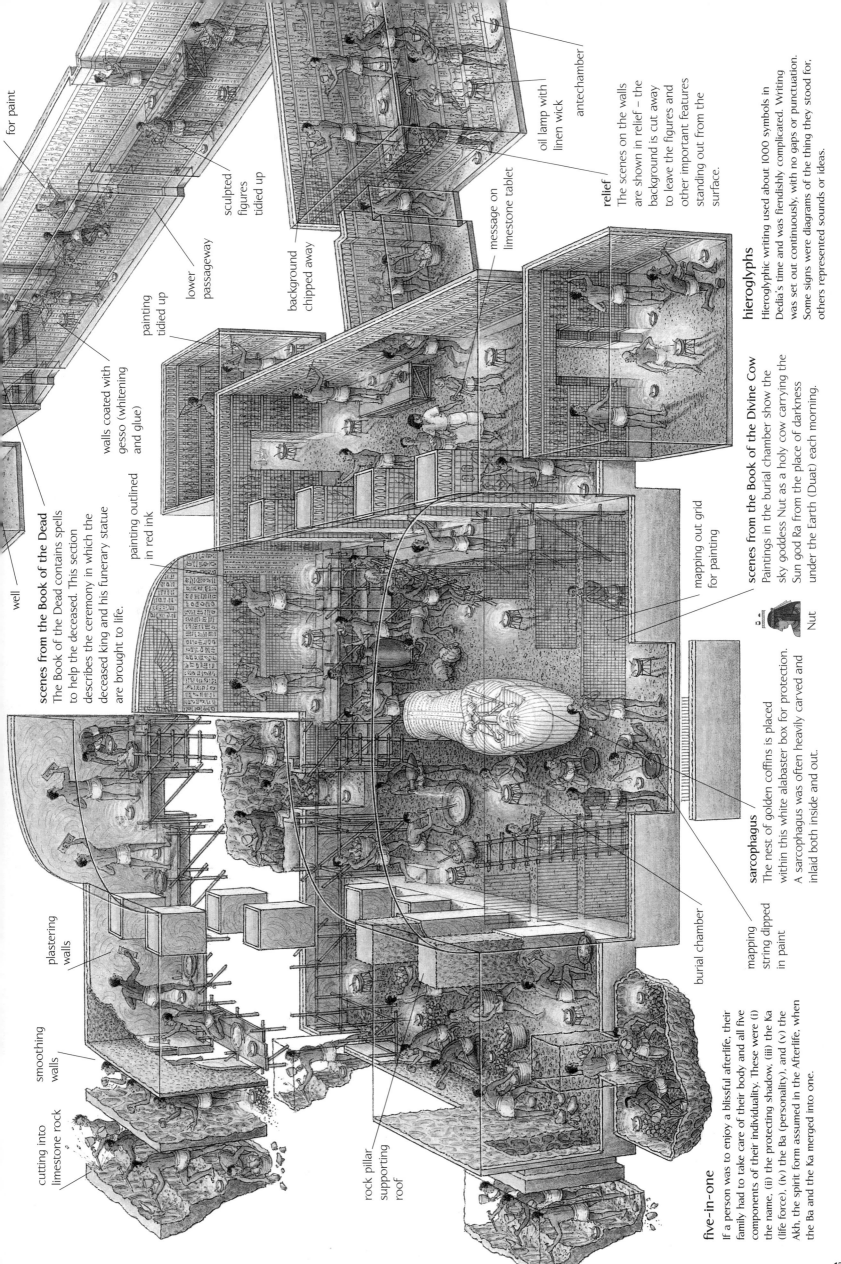

for paint

well

sculpted
figures
tidied up

painting
tidied up

lower
passageway

background
chipped away

message on
limestone tablet

oil lamp with
linen wick

antechamber

relief
The scenes on the walls
are shown in relief – the
background is cut away
to leave the figures and
other important features
standing out from the
surface.

hieroglyphs
Hieroglyphic writing used about 1000 symbols in
Dedia's time and was fiendishly complicated. Writing
was set out continuously, with no gaps or punctuation.
Some signs were diagrams of the thing they stood for,
others represented sounds or ideas.

scenes from the Book of the Dead
The Book of the Dead contains spells
to help the deceased. This section
describes the ceremony in which the
deceased king and his funerary statue
are brought to life.

walls coated with
gesso (whitening
and glue)

painting outlined
in red ink

mapping out grid
for painting

scenes from the Book of the Divine Cow
Paintings in the burial chamber show the
sky goddess Nut as a holy cow carrying the
Sun god Ra from the place of darkness
under the Earth (Duat) each morning.

Nut

plastering
walls

smoothing
walls

cutting into
limestone rock

burial chamber

mapping
string dipped
in paint

rock pillar
supporting
roof

sarcophagus
The nest of golden coffins is placed
within this white alabaster box for protection.
A sarcophagus was often heavily carved and
inlaid both inside and out.

five-in-one
If a person was to enjoy a blissful afterlife, their
family had to take care of their body and all five
components of their individuality. These were (i)
the name, (ii) the protecting shadow, (iii) the Ka
(life force), (iv) the Ba (personality), and (v) the
Akh, the spirit form assumed in the Afterlife, when
the Ba and the Ka merged into one.

17

Deir el-Medina stop-over

After the Valley of the Kings, Aunt Meritat was tired and Ipuia missed her lion cub. They returned to the boat with their servants, while Dad and I visited Deir el-Medina. We called on an old merchant friend of Dad's. He made us really welcome and insisted we stay the night. It was quite a relief to get away from Ipuia's running commentary on everyone and everything we saw.

toys
Egyptian children played with simple toys such as balls, dolls, spinning tops and model animals.

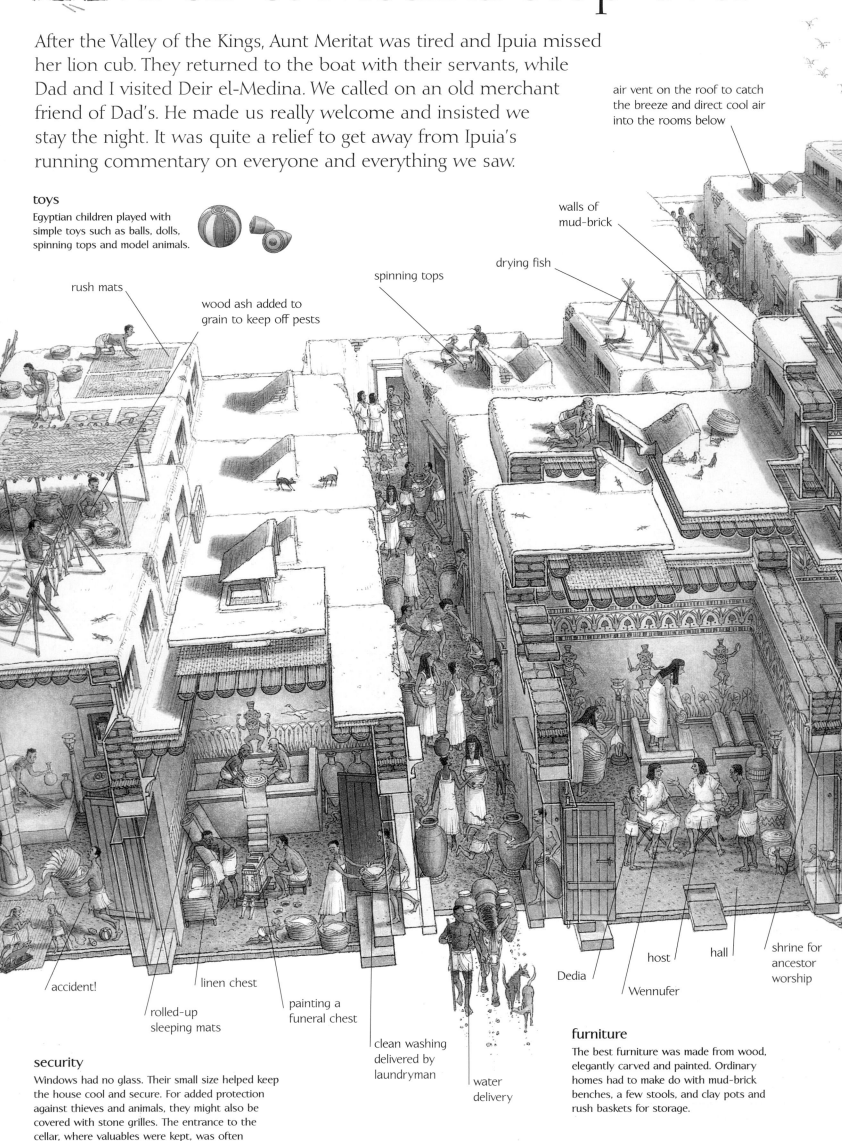

air vent on the roof to catch the breeze and direct cool air into the rooms below

walls of mud-brick

drying fish

spinning tops

rush mats

wood ash added to grain to keep off pests

accident!

linen chest

rolled-up sleeping mats

painting a funeral chest

clean washing delivered by laundryman

water delivery

Dedia

Wennufer

host

hall

shrine for ancestor worship

security
Windows had no glass. Their small size helped keep the house cool and secure. For added protection against thieves and animals, they might also be covered with stone grilles. The entrance to the cellar, where valuables were kept, was often protected by placing a bed over it.

furniture
The best furniture was made from wood, elegantly carved and painted. Ordinary homes had to make do with mud-brick benches, a few stools, and clay pots and rush baskets for storage.

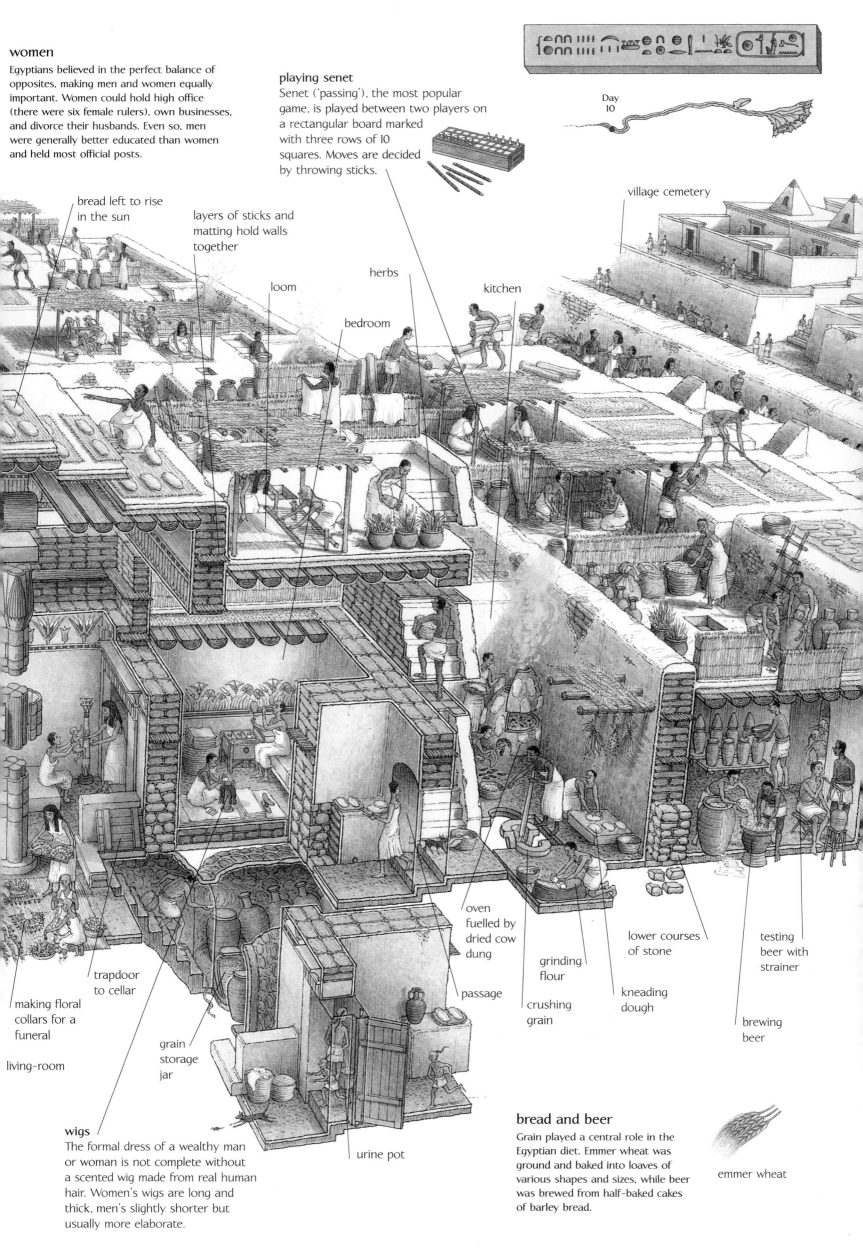

women

Egyptians believed in the perfect balance of opposites, making men and women equally important. Women could hold high office (there were six female rulers), own businesses, and divorce their husbands. Even so, men were generally better educated than women and held most official posts.

playing senet

Senet ('passing'), the most popular game, is played between two players on a rectangular board marked with three rows of 10 squares. Moves are decided by throwing sticks.

Day 10

bread left to rise in the sun

layers of sticks and matting hold walls together

loom

herbs

bedroom

kitchen

village cemetery

making floral collars for a funeral

living-room

trapdoor to cellar

grain storage jar

urine pot

oven fuelled by dried cow dung

passage

crushing grain

grinding flour

kneading dough

lower courses of stone

testing beer with strainer

brewing beer

wigs

The formal dress of a wealthy man or woman is not complete without a scented wig made from real human hair. Women's wigs are long and thick, men's slightly shorter but usually more elaborate.

bread and beer

Grain played a central role in the Egyptian diet. Emmer wheat was ground and baked into loaves of various shapes and sizes, while beer was brewed from half-baked cakes of barley bread.

emmer wheat

A funeral at Deir el-Medina

The next day Deir el-Medina held the funeral of its head man. As a mark of respect, Dad and I stayed to take part. The official's corpse had been prepared during the weeks since he had died. The priests organized the ceremony with meticulous detail. Everything that made him what he was – his body, soul, spirit, name and shadow – were cared for. He was sure to enjoy his next life.

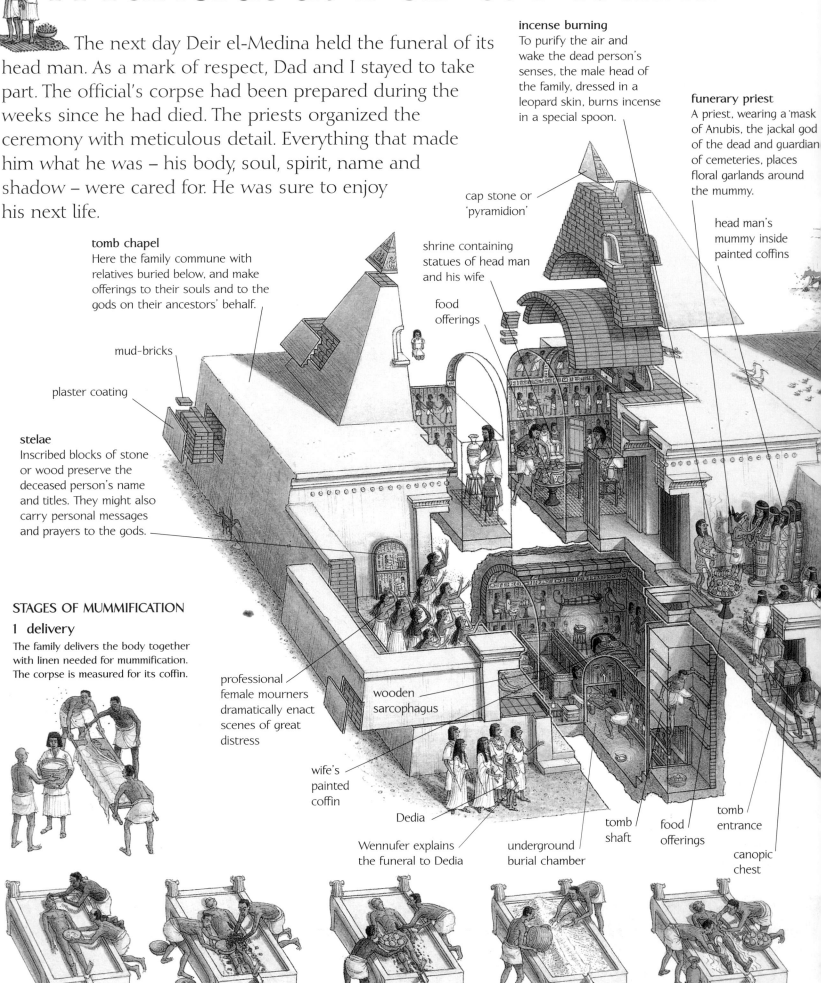

incense burning
To purify the air and wake the dead person's senses, the male head of the family, dressed in a leopard skin, burns incense in a special spoon.

funerary priest
A priest, wearing a 'mask of Anubis, the jackal god of the dead and guardian of cemeteries, places floral garlands around the mummy.

cap stone or 'pyramidion'

shrine containing statues of head man and his wife

food offerings

head man's mummy inside painted coffins

tomb chapel
Here the family commune with relatives buried below, and make offerings to their souls and to the gods on their ancestors' behalf.

mud-bricks

plaster coating

stelae
Inscribed blocks of stone or wood preserve the deceased person's name and titles. They might also carry personal messages and prayers to the gods.

professional female mourners dramatically enact scenes of great distress

wooden sarcophagus

wife's painted coffin

Dedia

Wennufer explains the funeral to Dedia

underground burial chamber

tomb shaft

food offerings

tomb entrance

canopic chest

STAGES OF MUMMIFICATION

1 delivery
The family delivers the body together with linen needed for mummification. The corpse is measured for its coffin.

2 de-braining
After the body has been laid out on a stone table, the brain is often removed through the nose with hooks. The inside of the skull is then washed out.

3 gutting
The corpse is cut open down the left side and the internal organs (except the heart and kidneys) are removed for separate preservation.

4 washing and stuffing
The body is washed with fragrant palm wine before the inner cavity is stuffed with water-absorbing natron and a temporary packing.

5 drying
To remove all vestiges of rot-inducing moisture, the body is covered with natron and left for 40 days.

6 cleaning and packing
Using Nile water, traces of natron are cleaned from the dried-out (desiccated) corpse. The empty body cavity is packed with sawdust and linen rags, and the head with resin-soaked linen.

journey to the Afterlife

In a final judgement after death, a person's heart was balanced against the feather of Maat (truth) to see if they were worthy of entering the Afterlife. The hearts of those who failed were flung to a hideous monster known as the 'Devourer'. Those who succeeded were allowed to proceed to the Field of Reeds, the kingdom of Osiris.

Day 11

grave goods
A dead person was provided with just about everything they might need in the next world, from clothes to jewellery.

villagers make their way to the funeral feast

clay seals
Often stamped with the image of Anubis, seals protect the locked doors to the tomb.

canopic chest
The corpse's internal organs (except the heart and kidneys, which are left in the body) have been mummified and stored in canopic jars. These are assembled in the canopic chest.

courtyard

white ox and sledge return to the village after delivering the coffin

friends and relatives, wearing white head bands, prepare to escort the body

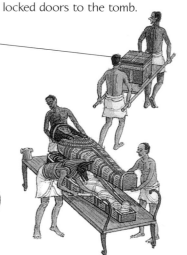

7 oiling
The body is transferred to a wooden table. Here its skin is rubbed with oils, the nose holes plugged, the eye sockets padded out, and a final coating of resin applied.

8 wrapping
Reciting spells at each stage, the embalmers start to bandage the body, beginning with the limbs.

9 protecting
In a process that takes many days, the entire corpse is wrapped in hundreds of metres of linen bandages. Protective amulets are placed within the bandaging.

10 securing
The well-wrapped corpse is secured with linen cords and placed within a linen shroud.

11 finishing
Adorned with a painted face mask, the body is lowered into its coffin. The jackal-headed priest places a papyrus Book of the Dead beside the body.

Saqqara's Step Pyramid

After Karnak, we sailed to Memphis to pick up a very important passenger: the regional governor. He was going to Piramesse to meet the king. As he wasn't ready when we arrived, we went on a sight-seeing trip to Saqqara, to visit the pyramid tombs of the ancient kings of Egypt. The massive repair works of Prince Khaemwaset made the place look a bit of a tip. Needless to say, Ipuia knew all about everything – except the ancient graffiti, which I found.

Step Pyramid
The first pyramid was built King Djoser. Starting as a mastaba, six massive 'steps' were added to create a pyramid 60 metres high.

pyramid restoration
By the time of Rameses II, the Saqqara pyramid complex was over 1000 years old. The king's fourth son, Khaemwaset, made a name for himself by restoring this and other monuments. It was a way of showing respect for his royal predecessors.

pyramid of King Unas

passage to burial chamber

burial chamber
The mummified body, its coffin and sarcophagus are laid deep in the burial chamber to keep them safe from robbers. The interior of King Unas's pyramid also contains the earliest-known pyramid texts – spells to help the deceased in various ways. Some of the texts were echoed in the later Book of the Dead.

mortuary temple
Deceased kings were gods. While alive, they built mortuary temples in which they could be worshipped after their death, and in which offerings could be made to sustain them in the next life.

pyramid construction
People have long wondered how pyramids were raised to such a height. The answer is probably that a massive ramp of earth, built alongside the pyramid site, was used to drag the building blocks into place.

injured worker
A construction-site doctor treats a worker with a broken arm. Egyptian doctors were skilled at dealing with fractures and similar injuries.

dead labourer

foreman

boat

boat pit of King Unas
As gods travel in holy barges, boats were buried near the king (who has become a god) for his use in the Afterlife.

supplies

causeway of Unas

relief carving

carpenters

workmen's camp and storage area

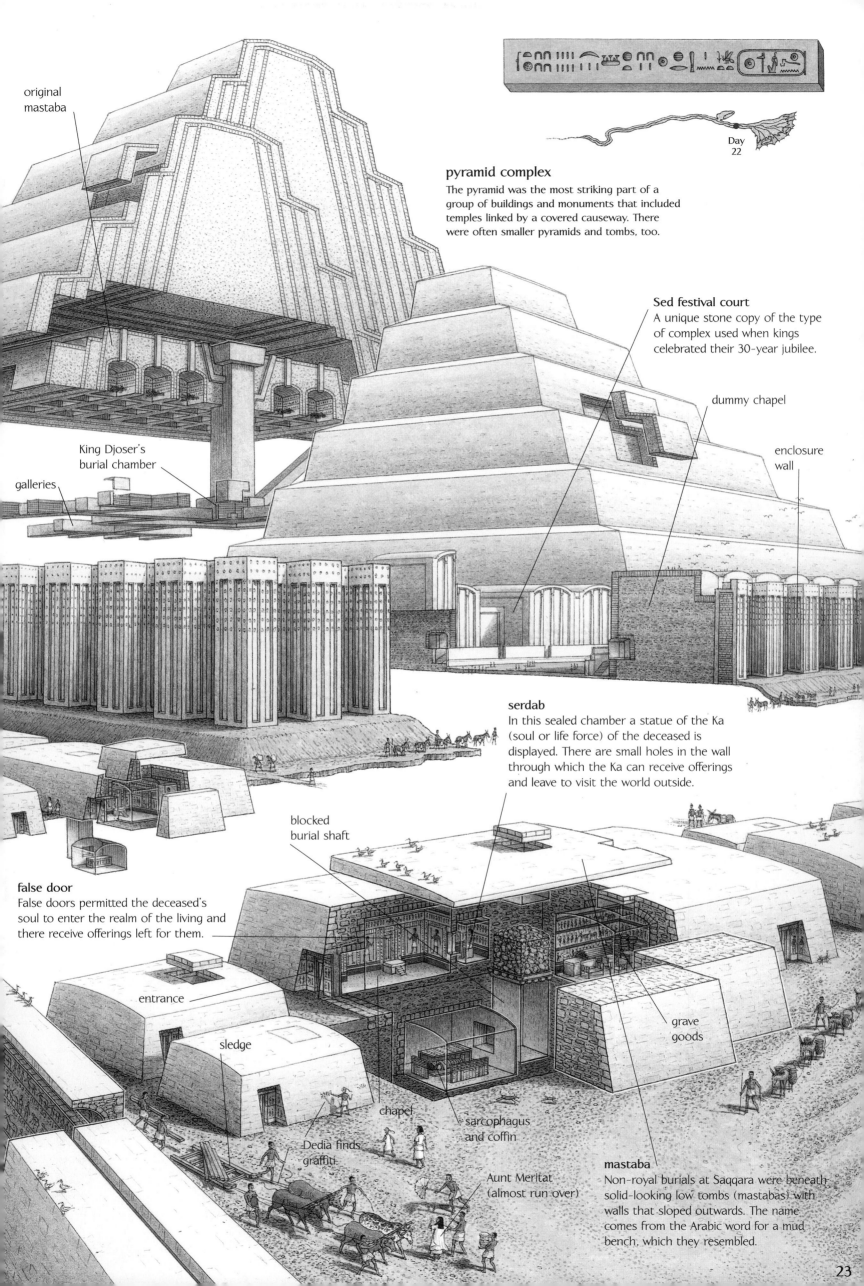

original mastaba

pyramid complex
The pyramid was the most striking part of a group of buildings and monuments that included temples linked by a covered causeway. There were often smaller pyramids and tombs, too.

Day 22

Sed festival court
A unique stone copy of the type of complex used when kings celebrated their 30-year jubilee.

dummy chapel

King Djoser's burial chamber

enclosure wall

galleries

serdab
In this sealed chamber a statue of the Ka (soul or life force) of the deceased is displayed. There are small holes in the wall through which the Ka can receive offerings and leave to visit the world outside.

blocked burial shaft

false door
False doors permitted the deceased's soul to enter the realm of the living and there receive offerings left for them.

entrance

grave goods

sledge

chapel

Dedia finds graffiti

sarcophagus and coffin

mastaba
Non-royal burials at Saqqara were beneath solid-looking low tombs (mastabas) with walls that sloped outwards. The name comes from the Arabic word for a mud bench, which they resembled.

Aunt Meritat (almost run over)

The fertile Nile

As we sailed on, I watched farmers recovering their fields and preparing them for sowing. One morning, as we were passing the pyramids and sphinx of Giza, the governor spoke to me. His Majesty, he said, was fond of animals. Would we like to offer him the lion cub? Without thinking, I said I'd be delighted. When I pointed out that it was Ipuia's, the governor smiled and said he'd settle things.

The Sphinx of Giza

'Sphinx' may have meant 'living image', and the largest and best-known example probably shows the face of King Khafra. 73 metres long and 20 metres high, it was originally carved from a single rocky outcrop. Workers are seen here replacing the Sphinx's beard.

marking out the fields

As the Inundation has washed away all the old field boundaries, they are measured out again by officials known as 'rope stretchers'.

villa

brick-making

Bricks are made with Nile mud reinforced with straw or chaff left over from threshing. They are not kiln-baked but simply left to dry out in the hot sun.

dried bricks

sowing

Wheat and barley are sown by scattering the seeds on the ground. They are then trampled in by goats.

trapping birds

Birds like wild duck and geese are a good source of meat. Hunting them is a popular sport, too.

ploughing

Because the flood soil is muddy and loose, teams of people or cows easily pull light wooden ploughs.

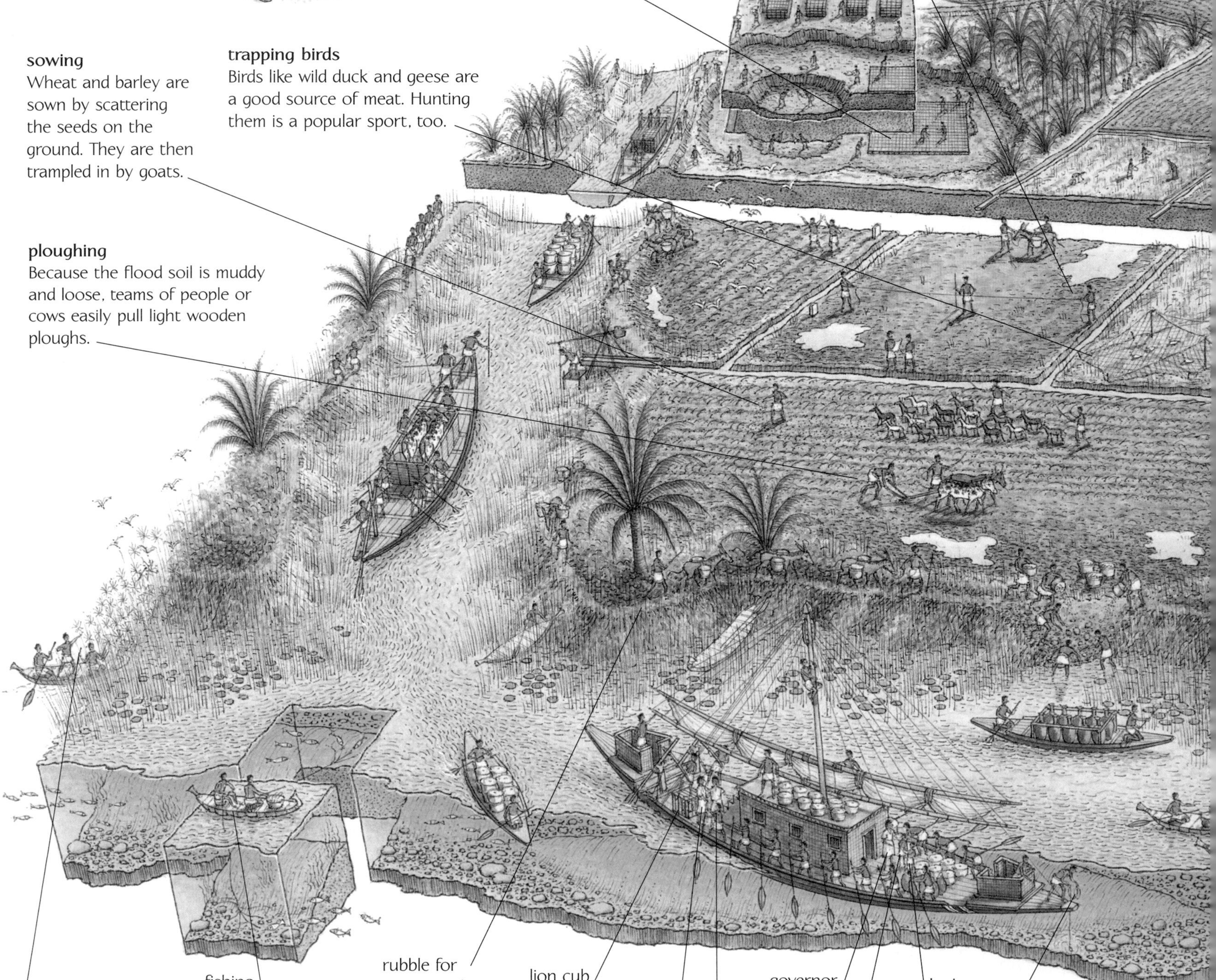

throwing stick

Birds are caught in nets or hunted with special wooden sticks that can be accurately thrown with great force.

fishing

rubble for repair work

lion cub

Wennufer

Aunt Meritat

governor

Dedia

Ipuia

the Inundation

Egypt was totally dependent on the annual flood (inundation) of the River Nile. This followed heavy rains in central Africa, far to the south, and left deposits of rich soil on either bank. Around Memphis the flood was highest in early September.

plumbing

A sailor checks the depth with a weight on the end of a plumb line. If a ship went aground when the river was falling, it might be stuck a long time!

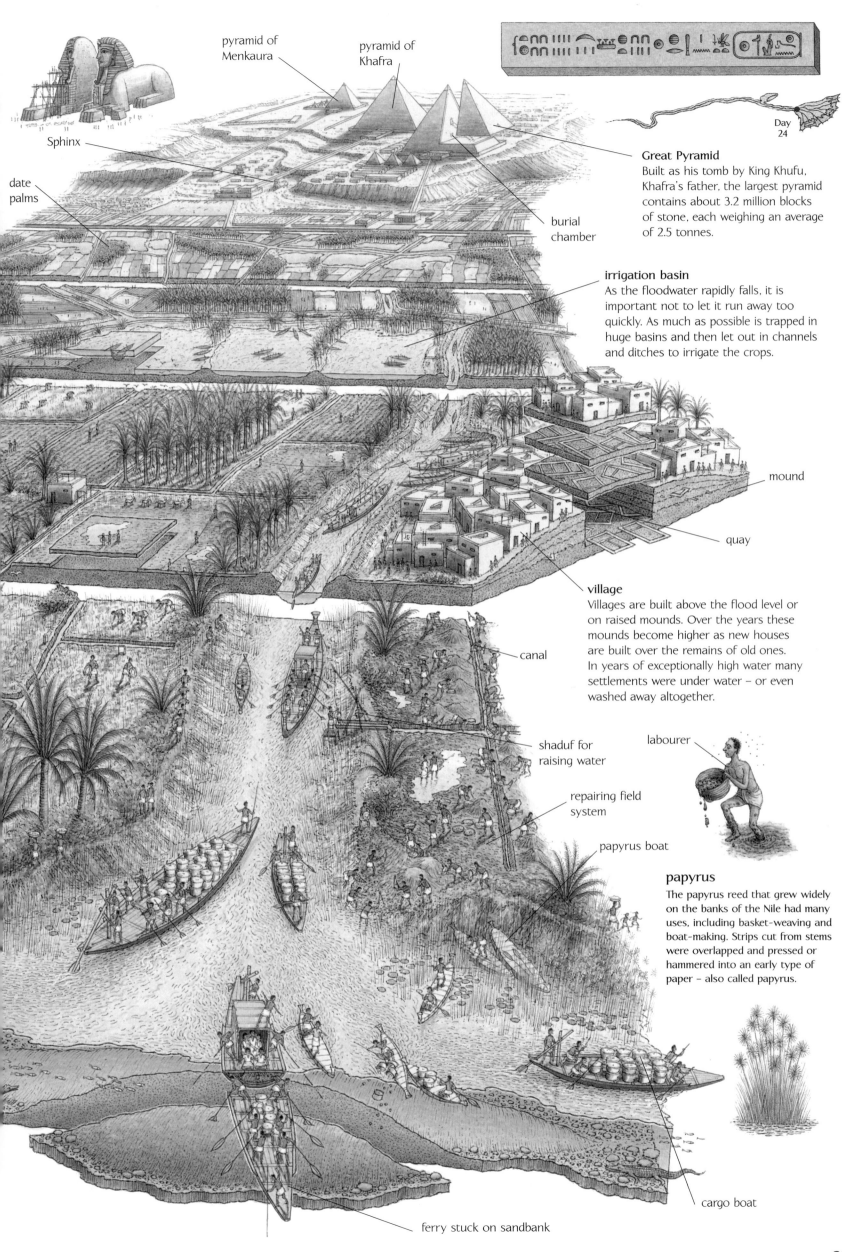

pyramid of Menkaura

pyramid of Khafra

Sphinx

date palms

burial chamber

Great Pyramid
Built as his tomb by King Khufu, Khafra's father, the largest pyramid contains about 3.2 million blocks of stone, each weighing an average of 2.5 tonnes.

irrigation basin
As the floodwater rapidly falls, it is important not to let it run away too quickly. As much as possible is trapped in huge basins and then let out in channels and ditches to irrigate the crops.

mound

quay

village
Villages are built above the flood level or on raised mounds. Over the years these mounds become higher as new houses are built over the remains of old ones. In years of exceptionally high water many settlements were under water – or even washed away altogether.

canal

shaduf for raising water

labourer

repairing field system

papyrus boat

papyrus
The papyrus reed that grew widely on the banks of the Nile had many uses, including basket-weaving and boat-making. Strips cut from stems were overlapped and pressed or hammered into an early type of paper – also called papyrus.

Day 24

cargo boat

ferry stuck on sandbank

25

Rameses's palace at Piramesse

How did the governor settle things with Ipuia? At Piramesse he arranged for us to present the lion cub to His Majesty *in person!* Walking through the palace courtyards, lying before the throne, hearing that voice – it was unforgettable. What's more, His Majesty presented Ipuia with a brilliant necklace. Afterwards, having shared so many adventures together, Ipuia and I actually became quite good friends. And we still are.

Rameses the Great

Rameses II is known as 'the Great' because, during his extraordinary 67-year reign, he constructed or took over a vast number and range of buildings (mostly in honour of Rameses II himself) all over Egypt.

throne room

The throne room is like the inner sanctuary of a temple, with the king-god himself seated on a raised platform at the far end.

pharaoh

The importance of the king's palace (*per-aa* or 'great house') is shown by the fact that the name eventually became the title of the king himself – pharaoh.

floor tiles

The floor tiles are decorated with images of the king's enemies so that everyone entering walks all over them!

instruments

The Egyptians loved music and played a variety of instruments: percussion (e.g. drums and tambourines), wind (e.g. flutes), and stringed (e.g. lutes).

pillared hall

The entire palace, but especially the pillared hall, is decorated with scenes that remind the viewer that the king is the source of fertility, wealth and plenty.

Day 30

daughter-wife
Bint Anath, the king's favourite wife (also his daughter), sits on his left.

fan-bearer

mud-plaster coating

rush matting

governor and lion cub

Wennufer

Dedia and Ipuia

26

tribute
Foreigners deliver tribute. Like other powerful kings, Rameses demands regular payment from the subject peoples within his widespread empire.

date palm

courtiers
The royal court was like a small village. It was populated by the royal family, high priests, nobles, scribes, officials, entertainers, guards and servants.

mandrake

ivory

palace pool
Complete with ducks, fish and water lilies, the pool is an echo of the sacredness of water in a barren land.

inlaid pavement

palm-style columns around courtyard

palace guard
Rameses can call on an enormous army of perhaps 20,000 soldiers. Only the élite, however, are selected to join his personal bodyguard.

gold

pomegranate
tree

ostrich

standard bearer

bugler

drummer

entertainment
Because their religion paid so much attention to death and rebirth, Egyptian civilization might be thought rather gloomy. Far from it! The royal court was alive with every type of delight, from dancing to board games, juggling and book collecting.

royal menagerie
Rameses was famous for his collection of wild animals (menagerie) – which really did include a lion cub!

baboons

Glossary

Afterlife: the Egyptians believed that death was just a transition between life on Earth and the Afterlife. Descriptions of the latter vary from people becoming stars to their continuing to live an Earth-style life in the fertile Field of Reeds.

Amduat: a text describing the nightly journey of the Sun through the Duat, the dark Underworld region beneath the Earth.

amulet: a small charm with magic or holy power, often in the shape of a sacred animal or object. It was worn to protect its owner or to give them special strength.

Book of Gates: a text guiding a deceased person through the complex network of doors and passageways of the Underworld to the chamber where they would be judged.

Book of the Dead: a collection of up to 190 spells, often written on papyrus and placed inside a coffin, to assist a deceased person in their quest to enter the Afterlife.

canopic jar: one of a set of four jars, stored within a canopic chest, in which were kept the preserved internal organs of a mummified body (except the heart and kidneys, which remained with the body).

cataract: rocky rapids that make a river impassable to boats.

hieroglyphs: Ancient Egypt's complex system of writing used three types of hieroglyphic symbol. Some were diagrams of the thing they represented, others represented sounds or ideas. Modern scholars could not read hieroglyphic writing until the discovery in 1799 and deciphering in 1822 of the Rosetta stone – an artefact inscribed with the same text in three languages, including hieroglyphs and the familiar ancient Greek.

hypostyle: a court filled with many pillars. These represented reeds growing around the mound from which the Earth had been made at the time of creation.

Inundation: the annual flooding of the Nile's banks as waters rushed down from the African highlands to the south. The Egyptians gave great religious significance to this seemingly miraculous event that brought life to an otherwise barren desert.

Ka: a person's life force – the key difference between them and an individual who had died. As long as it was fed and cherished, the Ka might live on after earthly death. When this happened, it also protected and nourished the deceased person's body.

mastaba: a solid-looking low tomb with outward-sloping walls. Some of the earliest royal burials were made beneath these bench-shaped structures.

natron: a compound of sodium that occurred in and around the sites of Egypt's prehistoric lakes. It was used for all kinds of cleaning purposes, most famously for drying out a corpse for mummification.

Nilometer: a device, often consisting of simple steps leading down to the water, by which the level of the River Nile was measured. It is not clear why this information was needed, but it seems to have been for religious, taxation or agricultural purposes.

obelisk: a needle-shaped stone monument connected to Sun worship. Baboons, famous for getting excited at sunrise, were often carved around the foot of an obelisk.

papyrus: a large, dense reed that grew beside the Nile and had many uses. It was woven into baskets and boats, and hammered into an early form of paper.

pharaoh: often used rather inaccurately to refer to any Egyptian ruler, pharaoh originally meant the royal palace ('per-aa' or 'great house'). By the middle of the 2nd millennium BCE, it was being used for the monarch (male or female) who occupied that house.

pigment: natural colouring which was mixed with oil or water to make paint or ink.

pylon: a huge, highly decorated gateway representing the pillars of the horizon through which the Sun rose each day. It comprised two tapering towers linked by a lower bridge-type construction.

pyramidion: a single pyramid-shaped stone placed at the top of a pyramid or obelisk. Many were gilded – covered in a thin layer of gold that shone in the rays of the Sun.

sarcophagus: a container, usually of stone, in which one or more coffins were stored for protection. The sarcophagus was normally carved and sometimes painted.

scribe: a respected professional writer who had mastered the complicated system of hieroglyphic writing.

senet: a popular game in which each player had seven pieces on a board of 30 squares in three rows of 10. Moves were determined by chance, and the object seems to have been to guide one's pieces along a twisting path – a bit like a sophisticated kind of snakes and ladders.

serdab: a room in a mastaba tomb where a statue of the deceased's Ka was usually placed. The chamber wall had one or more small openings for offerings to be passed in and through which the Ka could venture out.

shaduf: a device for lifting water that has been in use for thousands of years. The scoop on one end of a hinged pole is counterbalanced by a weight on the other.

shrine: an Egyptian temple was believed to be the place where a deity actually lived. The shrine was the inner chamber where their image was tended by priests.

sphinx: a creature with the head of a human or other animal, and the body of a lion. It was associated with the king and Sun worship.

stela: a stone or wood slab on which paintings, carvings or writings were displayed. They were often associated with caring for the dead.

tribute: payment made to a conquering power. When its empire was at its furthest extent, tribute poured into Egypt from all around the Near East.

Two Crowns: Egypt was once two kingdoms, Upper Egypt (south), represented by a white crown, and Lower Egypt (north), represented by a red crown. After the two were united around 3000 BCE, rulers could wear the double crown of Upper and Lower Egypt. The country itself was sometimes referred to as the 'Land of the Two Crowns'.

Underworld: known as the Duat, the Underworld was the dark region beneath the Earth through which the Sun sailed each night in a boat.

Kings and queens mentioned in the text

Djoser (2667–2648 BCE) was the king for whom the Step Pyramid at Saqqara was built.

Khufu (2589–2566 BCE) was the king who built the Great Pyramid of Giza.

Khafra (2558–2532 BCE), whose face is supposed to be on the Great Sphinx of Giza, was the son of Khufu.

Unas (2375–2345 BCE) was buried close to the Saqqara Step Pyramid.

Thutmose III (1479–1425 BCE), a successful warrior king, was buried in the Valley of the Kings.

Hatshepsut (1473–1458 BCE) was perhaps the most successful of all the women who ruled as pharaohs.

Rameses II (1279–1213 BCE) ruled for many years and built or took over a vast number of monuments, earning himself the title 'Rameses the Great'.

Bint-Anath (died around 1213 BCE) was Rameses II's eldest daughter, who later became his favourite queen.

Deities mentioned in the text

Amun-Ra: Amun, whose name may mean 'the hidden one', was a popular god of the Thebes region who became known as the 'king of the gods'. Sometimes shown with a ram's head, he was commonly linked to another popular and powerful deity, the Sun god Ra.

Anubis: the jackal-headed Anubis was god of the dead and guardian of cemeteries. Connected with mummification, his black colour was a reminder of the fertile soil found on the banks of the Nile.

Atum: an ancient creator god, Atum was also worshipped as a Sun god. Like Amun, he became closely linked with Ra, another Sun god.

Geb: a green-coloured god of the Earth, Geb, like Osiris, was responsible for vegetation.

Horus: the ancient falcon god Horus was a sky god and one of the protectors of Egypt's reigning king. Indeed, he was kingship itself in living form. His parents were the famous brother and sister lovers, Isis and Osiris.

Khnum: the ram god of Elephantine was linked to the Inundation, creativity and pottery.

Montu: another falcon-headed deity, Montu was the god of war.

Mut: Mut was the partner of Amun and holy mother of the ruling king. One of the daughters of the Sun, she was shown brightly clothed with a vulture head-dress.

Nut: Nut was the sky goddess whose body arched like the sky overhead. Some traditions said she swallowed the setting Sun every evening and gave birth to it again each morning. She was the sister-wife of the Earth god Geb.

Osiris: One of the earliest and most important Egyptian gods, Osiris was commonly shown as a royal mummy. He was associated with death, rebirth and fertility, and was commonly coloured green (vegetation) or black (soil). As the brother-partner of Isis, he fathered the falcon god Horus.

Index

OXFORD
UNIVERSITY PRESS

Great Clarendon Street, Oxford OX2 6DP

Oxford University Press is a department of the University of Oxford. It furthers the University's objective of excellence in research, scholarship, and education by publishing worldwide in

Oxford New York

Auckland Bangkok Buenos Aires Cape Town Chennai
Dar es Salaam Delhi Hong Kong Istanbul Karachi Kolkata
Kuala Lumpur Madrid Melbourne Mexico City Mumbai
Nairobi São Paulo Shanghai Taipei Tokyo Toronto

Oxford is a registered trade mark of Oxford University Press in the UK and in certain other countries

Illustrations © Stephen Biesty 2005
Text © Stewart Ross 2005

The moral rights of the author and illustrator have been asserted

Database right Oxford University Press (maker)

First published in 2005

British Library Cataloguing in Publication Data available

ISBN 0 19 911177 4

1 3 5 7 9 10 8 6 4 2

Printed in Italy